Fear?

NOT!

SHARLYNE CARLA

Copyright © 2020 Sharlyne Carla

All rights reserved. No part of this book may be reproduced or transmitted in any form or by any means, electronically or mechanically, including photocopying, recording, or by an information storage and retrieval system without permission in writing from the author of this book.

Scripture quotations are taken from the King James Version of the Holy Bible unless otherwise indicated.

ISBN: 978-1-7326199-2-0

Published by:

Spirit of Excellence
Writing & Editing Services, LLC

P.O. Box 608297, Orlando, FL 32860
www.TakeUpThySword.com

Edited by:
Dr. Ruth L. Baskerville
www.ruthbaskerville.com

Cover design by:
Jhonn de La Puente
jhonndelapuente@gmail.com

DEDICATION

This book is dedicated to every person who has been affected by the Coronavirus (COVID-19) pandemic. As we continue to pray for the families and friends who have lost loved ones and for those people who are currently fighting the infection in their own bodies, let's not allow the spirit of fear to distract us from thanking God for healing the survivors of this illness and for protecting all of us who are still trying to adjust to social distancing and other preventative measures.

TABLE OF CONTENTS

INTRODUCTION	6
WHO?	7
WHAT?	13
WHEN?	17
WHERE?	21
WHY?	25
CONCLUSION	29
ABOUT THE AUTHOR	30
CONTACT INFORMATION	31

Fear? NOT!

***Fear not*, for I am with thee, and will bless thee... Genesis 26:24b**

✝

INTRODUCTION

How many of you remember learning about the Five W's in school? I always had really good English teachers who made us read all of the American classics, and then we'd have to write thorough book reports. Answering these five questions was usually mandatory in developing a good paper: who? what? when? where? and why?

This book is about fear — but more importantly, the tools we need to be able to conquer any unhealthy, unproductive fears. We will be discussing the Five W's in relation to this topic. The Lord has helped me to overcome my own fears, many of which I will share with you in this book. Let's journey together to a place called Courage!

Be strong and courageous, do not fear nor be dismayed.
1 Chronicles 22:13b, AMP

Sharlyne Carla

But the Lord, who brought you up out of the land of Egypt with great power and a stretched out arm, him shall ye fear...
2 Kings 17:36

†

Who?

The scripture above is telling us exactly whom we should fear: God. But shouldn't we fear our enemies, frenemies or the devil himself? No, because verse 39 says that God will deliver us out of the hand of the enemy. And isn't our Lord — the creator of the heavens and the earth, the Alpha and the Omega — much bigger and far more powerful than anyone we could ever face? The fear of God I'm referring to is a reverential fear, which means that we should honor and respect His glory, majesty and lordship over us. Even the Son of God fears the Father according to scripture:

And the Spirit of the Lord will rest on Him—The Spirit of wisdom and understanding, The Spirit of counsel and strength, The Spirit of knowledge and of the [reverential and obedient] fear of the Lord—And He will delight in the fear of the Lord, And He will not judge by what His eyes see, Nor make decisions by what His ears hear. **Isaiah 11:2-3, AMP**

As Christians, we're supposed to follow the example of Christ; so if Jesus fears God, then we should too. And we know that after everything Jesus went through during His lifetime and crucifixion, He's definitely not afraid of anyone — human or demon. The scripture above also mentions that Jesus would have wisdom, understanding and knowledge. These three attributes are also related to the fear of God according to these passages:

And unto man he said, Behold, the fear of the Lord, that is wisdom; and to depart from evil is understanding. **Job 28:28**

The fear of the Lord is the beginning of wisdom: a good understanding have all they that do his commandments...
Psalm 111:10

The fear of the Lord is the beginning of wisdom: and the knowledge of the holy is understanding. **Proverbs 9:10**

We know that Jesus is not the only person mentioned in the Bible who feared God. Job 1:1 states that he "was perfect and upright, and one that feared God, and eschewed evil." Acts 10:22 describes Cornelius as "a just man, and one that feareth God, and of good report among all the nation of the Jews." And when the children of Israel were in slavery in Egypt and the lives of the newborn baby boys were threatened by Pharaoh, Exodus 1:17 said that "the midwives feared God, and did not as the king of Egypt commanded them, but saved the men children alive." All of these people were rewarded for fearing God as the Psalmist David reminds us:

Blessed is the man that feareth the Lord, that delighteth greatly in his commandments. **Psalm 112:1b**

He will bless them that fear the Lord, both small and great. **Psalm 115:13**

Blessed is every one that feareth the Lord; that walketh in his ways. **Psalm 128:1**

There was a time when I feared people more than God even though I had been in church all my life. I remember when I received my very first traffic ticket driving through Santa Monica, California, in 1991. That was the year I graduated from high school, and it was also the year that Rodney King was brutally beaten by police officers. I was literally scared for my life when highway patrol pulled me over. I was more afraid of being beaten or killed than I was of paying a fine or going to traffic school.

Unfortunately, our society appears to have gotten worse over the years in regard to racial tensions. But thanks be to God that Jesus Christ is the same yesterday, today and forever according to Hebrews 13:8. He is omnipotent (all-powerful), omniscient (all-knowing) and omnipresent (all-present). So even when we feel an initial fear come upon us as we encounter people such as bullies, bosses or bill collectors, we can always find peace, strength and courage in the Word of God:

Ye shall not fear them: for the Lord your God he shall fight for you. **Deuteronomy 3:22**

You, Lord, are the light that keeps me safe. I am not afraid of anyone. You protect me, and I have no fears. **Psalm 27:1, CEV**

The Lord is on my side; I will not fear: what can man do unto me? **Psalm 118:6**

Now that we know we're supposed to fear God and not man, we have a choice to make: We can hold on to our fears like 10 of the 12 men in Numbers 13 whom Moses sent out to search the land of Canaan, the land promised to God's people. Unlike Joshua and Caleb, they brought back a negative report about the inhabitants of that land being bigger and stronger than the children of

Israel. These men were so fearful that they saw themselves as grasshoppers compared to their enemies who were actual giants. Therefore, the Israelites had to remain in the wilderness for 40 years because they ignored this encouragement:

If the Lord delights in us, he will bring us into this land and give it to us, a land that flows with milk and honey. Only do not rebel against the Lord. And do not fear the people of the land, for they are bread for us. Their protection is removed from them, and the Lord is with us; do not fear them.

Numbers 14:8-9, ESV

Our alternative choice is to abandon the fear of man altogether like David did when faced his own giant, Goliath, in 1 Samuel 17. David was only a youth when he heard that killing this uncircumcised Philistine would result in riches, a wife and freedom for his entire family. This fateful encounter happened after the Prophet Samuel had anointed him to be the next king of Israel instead of Saul, but the people did not know it at the time. Before David addressed and defeated Goliath with no sword and no fear, he recounted the trials that God had already brought him through that gave him faith:

Your servant has struck down both lions and bears, and this uncircumcised Philistine shall be like one of them, for he has defied the armies of the living God. And David said, The Lord who delivered me from the paw of the lion and from the paw of the bear will deliver me from the hand of this Philistine...

1 Samuel 17:36-37, ESV

Jesus admonishes us in Matthew 10:28 that even with something as final and severe as death, we should not fear men because they can only kill our bodies. He tells us to fear God because He alone has the power to "destroy both soul and body in hell." I will conclude this chapter with some advice from King Solomon:

Let us hear the conclusion of the whole matter: Fear God, and keep his commandments: for this is the whole duty of man. **Ecclesiastes 12:13**

In God I will praise his word, in God I have put my trust; I will not fear what flesh can do unto me. Psalm 56:4

☦

What?

The scripture above is telling us exactly what we do not have to fear: mankind. Yes, that's a very broad term and encompasses so much. But if we examine all of the times that God tells us to "fear not" in the Bible, He is usually referring to people. So generally speaking, why shouldn't we fear others? Because verse 9 says that the Lord is on our side when we cry out to Him. He is a merciful and just God, and He will fight for the righteous. Here are a few reminders that our Father hears us:

If thou afflict them in any wise, and they cry at all unto me, I will surely hear their cry. ***Exodus 22:23***

He will fulfil the desire of them that fear him: he also will hear their cry, and will save them. ***Psalm 145:19***

You drew near on the day I called to You; You said, Fear not. ***Lamentations 3:57, AMPC***

We all like to quote Isaiah 54:17, which states that no weapon formed against us shall prosper. But how many of us run, duck and hide when those weapons actually form? I know that reaction all too well and can relate to some of these fearful illustrations: In relationships, we're afraid of someone lying to us, cheating on us or even worse, beating on us. At our jobs, we're afraid of someone firing us or demoting us. In school, we're afraid of someone picking on us or not picking us at all. So what can we do to combat these anticipated fears? Here is one passage that we should put to memory and pray out loud:

We are troubled on every side, yet not distressed; we are perplexed, but not in despair; Persecuted, but not forsaken; cast down, but not destroyed. ***2 Corinthians 4:8-9***

Since we mentioned weapons above, let's stay in this epistle and meditate on 2 Corinthians 10:4, which states, "the weapons of our warfare are not carnal." The Apostle Paul was reminding us that this is a spiritual battle and we need to fight to obtain and maintain a sound mind. Fears are birthed and nurtured in our minds, so we need to control our 'stinking thinking.' The New Life Version breaks it down this way:

We do not use those things to fight with that the world uses. We use the things God gives to fight with and they have power.

Those things God gives to fight with destroy the strong-places of the devil. We break down every thought and proud thing that puts itself up against the wisdom of God. We take hold of every thought and make it obey Christ. ***2 Corinthians 10:4-5***

Just like in the movies and in video games, there is a war going on between good and evil — in the natural and in the spirit. Satan wants to keep us in a state of fear because that is a form of bondage, oppression or isolation. But since "we are not ignorant of his devices" (2 Corinthians 2:11), we can stand on God's promises of victory:

And all this assembly shall know that the Lord saveth not with sword and spear: for the battle is the Lord's, and he will give you into our hands. ***1 Samuel 17:47***

Thus saith the Lord unto you, Be not afraid nor dismayed by reason of this great multitude; for the battle is not yours, but God's. ***2 Chronicles 20:15b***

With him is an arm of flesh; but with us is the Lord our God to help us, and to fight our battles... ***2 Chronicles 32:8***

If we know and serve the King of Glory — "the Lord strong and mighty, the Lord mighty in battle" (Psalm 24:8) — then what are we afraid of? How can we be "bold as a lion" according to Proverbs 28:1? Let's search the scriptures:

Fear? NOT!

What we may be afraid of	What God says about it in His Word
Apocalypse	And there shall be no more death, neither sorrow, nor crying, neither shall there be any more pain... **Revelation 21:4b**
Death	We are confident, and we would prefer to leave the body and to be at home with the Lord. **2 Corinthians 5:8, CEB**
Destiny	And we know that all things work together for good to them that love God, to them who are the called according to his purpose. **Romans 8:28**
Disappointment	Trust in the Lord with all thine heart; and lean not unto thine own understanding. **Proverbs 3:5**
Embarrassment	Humble yourselves therefore under the mighty hand of God, that he may exalt you in due time. **1 Peter 5:6**
Ignorance	If any of you lack wisdom, let him ask of God, that giveth to all men liberally... **James 1:5**
Lack	Those who trust in the Lord will lack no good thing. **Psalm 34:10b, NLT**
Loneliness	I will never leave thee, nor forsake thee. **Hebrews 13:5**
Rejection	He made us accepted in the Beloved. **Ephesians 1:6b, NKJV**
Shame	For your shame ye shall have double... **Isaiah 61:7**
Sickness	And with his stripes we are healed. **Isaiah 53:5b**
Suffering	In the world ye shall have tribulation: but be of good cheer; I have overcome the world. **John 16:33b**
Theft	Vengeance is mine; I will repay, saith the Lord. **Romans 12:19**

Sharlyne Carla

When thou goest out to battle against thine enemies, and seest horses, and chariots, and a people more than thou, be not afraid of them... Deuteronomy 20:1

✝

WHEN?

The scripture above is telling us exactly when we should not fear: during war. Of course, everyone's war is different and does not necessarily have to involve an actual international conflict involving guns and bloodshed. For the purposes of this book, 'war' refers to any type of struggle, fight, attack, hostility, strife, discord or confrontation that we may encounter — whether it's physical, spiritual, emotional, mental or even financial. Verse 3 tells us to "fear not" and here's why:

For the Lord your God is he who goes with you to fight for you against your enemies, to give you the victory.

Deuteronomy 20:4, ESV

Remember in Genesis 3:15 when God said that He would put enmity (opposition) between Eve and the serpent as well as their descendants? That is why we have an ongoing war today, which many Christians refer to as spiritual warfare. We know that 'life happens' and we all have our own cross to bear. The key is to be proactive instead of reactive — we should not just wait around for the enemy (or even fate) to disrupt our peaceful, joyful existence. If the real soldiers go out to war in special tactical gear, then we should also dress the part every day:

Wherefore take unto you the whole armour of God, that ye may be able to withstand in the evil day, and having done all, to stand. Stand therefore, having your loins girt about with truth, and having on the breastplate of righteousness; And your feet shod with the preparation of the gospel of peace; Above all, taking the shield of faith, wherewith ye shall be able to quench all the fiery darts of the wicked. And take the helmet of salvation, and the sword of the Spirit, which is the word of God.

Ephesians 6:13-17

The reason why we are instructed in 1 Thessalonians 5:17 to "pray without ceasing" is because we need to be ready when our individual wars come. I once heard a pastor say that each person is perpetually in one of three stages: about to go into a storm, currently in a storm or finally coming out of a storm. However, that does not give us a free pass to remain in a constant state of fear because of our past, present or possible future trials. Here are some scriptures to keep close by:

When you lie down, you will not be afraid; you will lie down, and your sleep will be pleasant. **Proverbs 3:24, CSB**

Be not afraid of sudden fear, neither of the desolation of the wicked, when it cometh. **Proverbs 3:25**

I am not afraid in times of danger when I am surrounded by enemies. **Psalm 49:5, GNT**

Having walked this earth for nearly five decades, I have been through my fair share of trials, including when I got divorced (twice), when I got laid off (twice), and when I lost my first home after 12 years. One of the hardest times was in 2017 because not only was I going through foreclosure, I was paying thousands of dollars to fix a car (that I later gave away); attending college to obtain a master's degree (20 years after getting a bachelor's degree); and studying to be licensed as an insurance agent (which I never planned on nor desired). Was I afraid at times? I most certainly was. But like the Apostle Paul, I had to decree and declare these three simple words from Acts 27:25b:

I believe God...

We all have the right to be afraid when we're going through our personal wars; however, we cannot let that fear paralyze us from moving forward in our purpose or prevent us from trusting God to deliver us. When the three Hebrew boys survived the fiery furnace, we learned that "there is no other God that can deliver after this sort" (Daniel 3:29). When Daniel survived the lions' den, it was "because he believed in his God" (Daniel 6:23). And when the Prophet Elijah defeated the 450 prophets of Baal, even the unbelievers had to declare, "The Lord, he is the God" (1 Kings 18:39). In all of these situations, I can hear the Lord saying:

> War a good warfare; Holding faith, and a good conscience...
> 1 Timothy 1:18b-19

As we can see, there is usually a method to the madness caused by our hardships. We can transform our fear into faith by knowing that our Father will turn our mess into a message and our test into a testimony after we have suffered awhile according to 1 Peter 5:10. And while we're waiting, we can stand on this Word:

> When the enemy shall come in like a flood, the Spirit of the Lord shall lift up a standard against him. Isaiah 59:19b

Sharlyne Carla

There they were, in much fear, where there was nothing to be afraid of...
Psalm 53:5, NLV

WHERE?

The scripture above is telling us exactly where we should fear: nowhere. In the Holman KJV Study Bible, this Psalm is titled "The Ungodly Man's Fear of the Lord" because it's talking about a fool who doesn't believe in God. That does sound a little strange considering the fact that verse 6 reveals the future deliverance of God's people. Whenever we find ourselves in a place where it appears that the Lord has abandoned us, we cannot succumb to fear. Remember that our Father will always ensure that we have a safe place to go:

In the fear of the Lord is strong confidence: and his children shall have a place of refuge. **Proverbs 14:26**

And there shall be a tabernacle for a shadow in the day time from the heat, and for a place of refuge, and for a covert from storm and from rain. **Isaiah 4:6**

I will bring them again unto this place, and I will cause them to dwell safely. **Jeremiah 32:37b**

Sometimes we find ourselves in a place — physically or emotionally — where we may feel a little scared, very frightened or hopelessly anxious. It is in these places where we must seek God and know that He's there with us and ready to bring us out of any undesirable location or circumstance. Let's see how Jonah got out of his tight situation:

Then Jonah prayed unto the Lord his God out of the fish's belly, And said, I cried by reason of mine affliction unto the Lord, and he heard me; out of the belly of hell cried I, and thou heardest my voice. **Jonah 2:1-2**

King David was so confident that God could reach him anywhere that he wrote in Psalm 139:8 that the Lord could be with him both in heaven and in hell. And of course, we're more than welcome to dwell "in the secret place of the most High" according to Psalm 91:1. When we end up in a fearful state, the question is not, "Where is God?" The real question is, "Where is your faith?" (Luke 8:25). This is where your faith should be:

in God Mark 11:22
in His Name Acts 3:16
in His Blood Romans 3:25
in Christ Jesus Galatians 3:26

Abraham is referred to as 'the father of faith,' and one of the reasons is that he simply obeyed and believed God. On two specific occasions, Abraham just blindly went where the Lord told him to go. In Genesis 12:1, God said, "Get thee out of thy country, and from thy kindred, and from thy father's house, unto a land that I will shew thee." And in Genesis 22:2, God said, "Get thee into the land of Moriah; and offer him there for a burnt offering upon one of the mountains which I will tell thee of." Both times, Abraham simply decided to go — he didn't have a map or GPS, just a Word from the Lord. I have learned from Joyce Meyer to 'do it afraid.' We can move forward from where we are whether or not we have an exact destination:

Fear not to go down into Egypt; for I will there make of thee a great nation. **Genesis 46:3b**

Behold, the Lord thy God hath set the land before thee: go up and possess it, as the Lord God of thy fathers hath said unto thee; fear not, neither be discouraged. **Deuteronomy 1:21**

And the Lord said unto Joshua, Fear not, neither be thou dismayed: take all the people of war with thee, and arise, go up to Ai... **Joshua 8:1**

In 1994, God used the Northridge earthquake in California to move me across the country to Rhode Island. I always tell people, "I cannot live in fear," and that is why I left my hometown of Pomona. To me, earthquakes are the scariest natural disaster because we can't predict them. So the Lord used my fear to start me on a nine-year journey northeast, then south to Orlando, Florida, and eventually to true salvation, sanctification and communion with the Holy Spirit. What's funny is that I wasn't afraid to make two out-of-state moves — one by myself and the other with my daughter. God brought me exactly where I needed to be without me even knowing that He was in the driver's seat the entire time. Now I know firsthand that this passage of scripture is true:

But [he] made his own people to go forth like sheep, and guided them in the wilderness like a flock. And he led them on safely, so that they feared not: but the sea overwhelmed their enemies.

Psalm 78:52-53

Jesus answered, Why are you afraid? You don't have enough faith... Matthew 8:26, ERV

WHY?

The scripture above is telling us exactly why we fear: faithlessness. When Christ Himself tells us that we don't have enough faith, then it's time to go back to the drawing board. There's a reason why we sometimes let our faith be overshadowed by our fears. The 'b' part of the verse above is the main reason why we don't have to be afraid: Jesus has the power to calm every storm. And because He is the vine and we are the branches according to John 15:5, we can stand on this Word:

Behold, I give unto you power to tread on serpents and scorpions, and over all the power of the enemy: and nothing shall by any means hurt you. **Luke 10:19**

Let's look at another story about Jesus and His disciples out on the water. In the 14th chapter of the Book of Matthew, Jesus is literally walking on water but His disciples are afraid instead of amazed. Like many of us, they're afraid of the unknown — Is it Christ or a spirit? When Peter casts his fear aside and decides to get out of the boat to walk on the water to Jesus simply because He said "come," this is the outcome:

But when he saw the wind boisterous, he was afraid; and beginning to sink, he cried, saying, Lord, save me. And immediately Jesus stretched forth his hand, and caught him, and said unto him, O thou of little faith, wherefore didst thou doubt? **Matthew 14:30-31**

Like many of us, Peter started out on the path of confidence and faith until the road got a little rocky and he began to look at his circumstances and lose his focus on the One who could deliver him. Aren't we supposed to walk by faith and not by sight (2 Corinthians 5:7)? Then why do we let fear get the best of us when we know that we serve a mighty God? We should meditate on these passages more often:

Is any thing too hard for the Lord? **Genesis 18:14a**

Ah Lord God! behold, thou hast made the heaven and the earth by thy great power and stretched out arm, and there is nothing too hard for thee. **Jeremiah 32:17**

The things which are impossible with men are possible with God. **Luke 18:27b**

When our children ask us if they can go somewhere or do something that we don't think is best for them and we say no and they ask why, don't we usually reply: "Because I said so!" Well just imagine asking our Father if we can be afraid of something or someone and He says no and we ask why and He replies: "Because I said so!" Here's a little bit of what that looks like in His Word:

Fear not, nor be afraid of them: for the Lord thy God, he it is that doth go with thee; he will not fail thee, nor forsake thee.	Deuteronomy 31:6
Fear not, nor be dismayed, be strong and of good courage: for thus shall the Lord do to all your enemies against whom ye fight.	Joshua 10:25
Fear not: thou shalt not die.	Judges 6:23
Fear not: for they that be with us are more than they that be with them.	2 Kings 6:16
Fear not, nor be dismayed: for the Lord God, even my God, will be with thee; he will not fail thee, nor forsake thee, until thou hast finished all the work for the service of the house of the Lord.	1 Chronicles 28:20
Fear not: behold, your God will come with vengeance, even God with a recompence; he will come and save you.	Isaiah 35:4
Fear not; I will help thee.	Isaiah 41:13
Fear not; for thou shalt not be ashamed...	Isaiah 54:4
Fear not: peace be unto thee, be strong, yea, be strong...	Daniel 10:19
Fear not, O land; be glad and rejoice: for the Lord will do great things.	Joel 2:21
Fear not, but let your hands be strong.	Zechariah 8:13
Fear not therefore: ye are of more value than many sparrows.	Luke 12:7
Fear not, little flock; for it is your Father's good pleasure to give you the kingdom.	Luke 12:32

There are countless stories of healings throughout the Bible but very few resurrections from the dead. While Jesus was in the midst of concurrently healing various people, He heard that the 12-year-old girl He was on the way to see had just died. The first thing Jesus said to the young girl's father was, "Fear not: believe only, and she shall be made whole" (Luke 8:50). What if that father allowed the fear of hearing about his child's death to override the faith he needed in Jesus to not only heal her but to actually raise her from the dead? Faith and fear cannot coexist, so we must trust that God's Word is true:

But now thus saith the Lord that created thee, O Jacob, and he that formed thee, O Israel, Fear not: for I have redeemed thee, I have called thee by thy name; thou art mine. When thou passest through the waters, I will be with thee; and through the rivers, they shall not overflow thee: when thou walkest through the fire, thou shalt not be burned; neither shall the flame kindle upon thee. **Isaiah 43:1-2**

Sharlyne Carla

***Fear not**, and be not dismayed; tomorrow go out against them, and the Lord will be with you. 2 Chronicles 20:17b, RSV*

CONCLUSION

It has been quite a journey, but I do believe that we have reached that place called Courage! Because we believe every word in the Bible from Genesis to Revelation, we know that God did not give us the spirit of fear (2 Timothy 1:7). And we know that fear involves torment (1 John 4:18). But let's remember most of all that once we utterly destroy our fears, like an adversary, we won't see them ever again (Exodus 14:13).

I have learned to turn my fears into fuel to power my attack against the enemy's camp even before any fiery darts are thrown at me. I have learned to hold on to God's unchanging hand even while I'm crying from the pain of the crushing that is meant to release the anointing oil over my life. Let's all learn to be more courageous:

Be strong and of a good courage; be not afraid, neither be thou dismayed: for the Lord thy God is with thee whithersoever thou goest. ***Joshua 1:9b***

ABOUT THE AUTHOR

Sharlyne C. Rogers (formerly Sharlyne C. Thomas), writing as **Sharlyne Carla**, is a professional editor, inspirational speaker, and award-winning author who has published six other non-fiction books thus far. She holds an MBA in Management, a BS in Paralegal Studies, and a Florida Woman & Minority Business Certification. As the Managing Member of Spirit of Excellence Writing & Editing Services, LLC, Sharlyne has contributed articles to periodicals such as *IBA Success Magazine* and *Built to Prosper* while editing and proofreading various copy for a broad range of writers and organizations nationwide.

Sharlyne has been invited to speak and teach at a variety of community and ministry events, including Destined for Destiny Women's Institute and the Central Florida Mayors' Prayer Breakfast. She has also judged four business/beauty pageants and has been a guest on several radio and TV shows such as WOKB 1680AM, Rejoice 1140AM, *Point of View* on the Afrotainment Channel, and *Atlanta Live* on WATC-TV 57.

Sharlyne is also the Founder of Sword of the Spirit Ministries Florida, Inc., a 501c3 nonprofit charity organization that empowers single parents and their children to become more productive citizens spiritually, physically, and financially. Born and raised in Southern California, she currently lives with her husband William in Central Florida.

Sharlyne Carla

CONTACT INFORMATION

Sharlyne Carla, Kingdom Ambassador
FB: @takeupthysword · IG: @sharlynecarla
sharlynecarla@gmail.com
321-209-2309

Please feel free to contact the author with any questions, comments, or prayer requests. She is available for book club presentations, signings, and speaking engagements for your business or church, including special events, workshops, conferences, retreats, and seminars. Other works by the author can be purchased at www.TakeUpThySword.com:

www.ingramcontent.com/pod-product-compliance
Lightning Source LLC
Chambersburg PA
CBHW070120110526
44587CB00016BA/2735